To:

From:

Date:

a collection of stories,
quotes, scriptures,
and inspirational thoughts

a T☉uch

of love to say congratulations

HOWARD
PUBLISHING CO.

A Touch of Love to Say Congratulations © 2002 by Howard Publishing Company
All rights reserved. Printed in Mexico

Published by Howard Publishing Co., Inc.,
3117 North 7th Street, West Monroe, LA 71291-2227

Contributors: Angie Kiesling, Ginger Young, Chrys Howard, Debbie Webb,
Gary Myers, Philis Boultinghouse

02 03 04 05 06 07 08 09 10 11   10 9 8 7 6 5 4 3 2 1

Edited by Philis Boultinghouse
Concept and design by Steve Diggs and Friends, Nashville

ISBN: 1-58229-228-0

Our purpose at Howard Publishing is to:
- *Increase faith* in the hearts of growing Christians
- *Inspire holiness* in the lives of believers
- *Instill hope* in the hearts of struggling people everywhere

Because He's coming again!

A Touch of Love to Say
Congratulations

Celebration

Outstanding

Number One

Gratitude

Remembrance

Affirmation

Treasure

Success

CHAPTER 1

Celebration

Accomplishments, fulfilled dreams, unexpected awards, quantum "life leaps"—they're all reason to celebrate, and here's a wish to get your celebration off to a big start:

May God bless you and keep you.

May He multiply your endeavors and fill up your "joy reservoir."

May God use this happy event to remind you of His presence—and continual goodness—in your life.

Congratulations!

PSALM 68:3

May the righteous

be glad and rejoice

before God; may they

be happy and joyful.

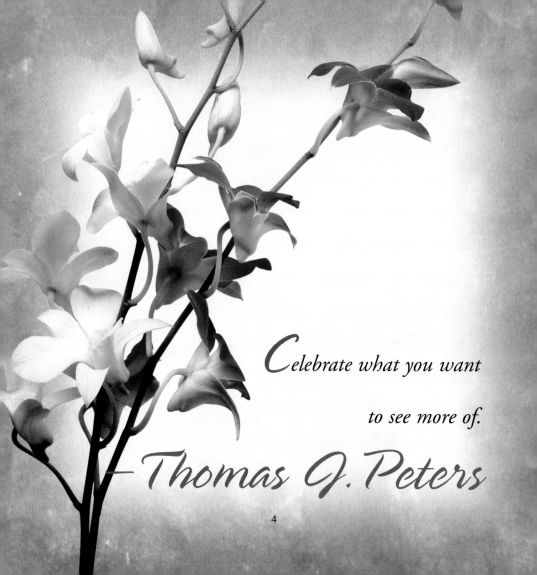

Celebrate what you want

to see more of.

— Thomas J. Peters

Learning to Read

To Jodi, the letters all ran together on the page. Sometimes she could distinguish between them, sometimes she couldn't. Lower case *p*s, *b*s, and *d*s really confused her, not to mention *m*s and *n*s. Even *i*s and *t*s could get inverted. But with *w*s and *v*s, she could never make a distinction. Why did learning to read have to be so difficult?

Ever since she could remember, Jodi had wanted to read. Her mother read books to her several times a day before she started school, her daddy read to her at bedtime, and her older brother, Jase, read her "chapter books." That was the most impressive thing of all to Jodi: Jase could read "chapter books." She had no greater aspiration in life than to read like that.

Six-year-old Jodi Spencer had been enthralled with books as a toddler, and her fascination had increased over time until it had become an obsession. Her bedroom was a testimony to her love for

Chapter One: *Celebration*

books. There were books on her dresser, books in her closet, books by her bed, books in shelves lining her walls. Jodi kept a stash of books in the backseat of the car and in the purse that dangled off her arm. She made sure that she never got caught in a situation where there were no books.

The fact that most of Jodi's books were storybooks with more pictures than words hadn't mattered to her until she entered first grade. She had memorized the ones her family read to her time and time again. She kept those priceless treasures on a special shelf near her bed and dragged them out when she needed a little boost in her spirits. She loved the feeling of the carefully crafted words rolling off her tongue, usually in rhyme. But in the hidden places of her heart, Jodi harbored an intense longing to be able to grasp the words with her eyes and her mind from off the page, rather than from her memory. She ached to consume and comprehend entire books without having any help and without that stuttering feeling in her head.

That was the best description Jodi had for what happened inside when she tried to read. The letters seemed to get cluttered and congested and she felt a stuttering sensation that clogged her brain with confusion.

Jodi's mom had met with her teacher on several occasions to discuss the dilemma. Twice, a teacher whom Jodi had never seen before came to her class and took her to a small room for some special tests to determine what the problem might be. Jodi sensed their concern, but she refused to be discouraged. Jodi would go home every day and crawl up on her bed with one of the books she had memorized and "read" until her heart was content.

All of Jodi's classmates were reading by now—some slowly, some exceptionally well—but all of them were reading. Eventually, Jodi caught on to the fact that she was the only one in the class who wasn't, and it was breaking her heart. She felt a heaviness in her spirit that was taking a toll on her enthusiasm for learning.

The Spencers contracted a tutor who specialized in reading disabilities. She was a very nice lady, but she and Jodi couldn't seem to nail down the problem. Her patience with Jodi helped her feel better, but after three months of tutoring, her reading hadn't improved. The tutor stopped coming.

Chapter One: *Celebration*

Eleven-year-old Jase Spencer loved his little sister. She had always had such a joyful way about her. And Jase especially loved her generosity and compassion. She was very thoughtful of him. When her physician would give her a sucker, she would always ask, "Can I have one for my brother?" In fact, if she couldn't get him one, she would save hers for him. She particularly loved to buy him gumballs when she accompanied her mother to the grocery store and had coins to spend.

Jodi often came into his room to console him when he was in trouble with Mom or Dad. She would sneak in when they weren't looking, bringing a Popsicle or a book to read to him. She would speak tender words to bolster his fragile male ego and rub his back as she spoke, unaware that she was contributing a vital element of strength to his self-esteem. It was an intuitive response born of love and admiration. Jodi revered her big brother.

Even at his young age, Jase knew that Jodi's way with words was unique. Her verbiage reflected her passion for words. He was sure that she would be a poet or a novelist. She derived such delight from putting phrases together like puzzles, each word fitting snugly against the one before it with some twist that connected each to the other. She strung thoughts together with ease and impressive skill.

One night as Jase was passing Jodi's room in the hallway, he heard a whimpering sound seeping out from under the door. He walked in softly and discovered his little sister facedown on her bed, surrounded by her books, weeping. "Jode," he started, "what's wrong?"

"Oh Jase, I'm never gonna learn to read, am I?" Jodi sobbed.

Jase's heart wrenched. He had ventured that same question a couple of times when overhearing the sober discussions his parents whispered behind her back. "Sure you are, sis," Jase responded. "With some kids, it just takes longer than others, but you will read. I guarantee you that."

"How can you be so sure, Jase?" Jodi begged.

"Cause I'm your brother, and nobody knows you like I do," he replied assuredly.

"But Jase, my teacher has tried to help me, Mom and Dad have tried, and that tutor tried. Nobody can help me, Jase. I'm scared I'm never gonna read." Jodi broke into a wail at those last words, the despair in her heart giving full expression.

"Yeah, but *I* haven't tried yet, Jodi. And there's nothing I can't do," Jase said in his most confident tone of voice. "I'm fixin' to start helping you, and you're *gonna* read."

Chapter One: *Celebration*

Now that the words had come out of his mouth, he had no choice but to act on them. Besides, he knew his determined little sister. She was relentless when she wanted something, and there was nothing she wanted as badly as she wanted to read.

"Jase, are you for real? I mean, do you really think you can do it?" Jodi's voice was hopeful.

"Yep!" Jase said. "In fact, let's get started."

"Should we start with one of these books?" Jodi asked.

"Nope!" Jase responded. "We're gonna use one of my books."

Jase disappeared into his room and returned with one of his favorites, *The Adventures of Hank, the Cowdog*. Jodi's eyes lit up! It was a chapter book!

Night after night, Jase and Jodi stole away into one of their rooms and pored over old Hank, the cowdog, and his comical adventures. Word by word, they labored, reading and rereading—over and over. Weeks went by, then months. Some nights the two of them laughed so hard at the antics of the redneck canine that they forgot they were working; other nights they got so frustrated over Jodi's difficulty that they would end up yelling at each other and she would run to her room in tears. Jase would weary of the work, but Jodi nagged him with his promise, reminding him that he "guaranteed" that she would read.

Finally, one day just after spring had dawned, Jase and Jodi called their mom and dad into the den for a special surprise. Jodi sat perched on a stool, dressed in her favorite outfit. Her long, curly hair was pulled back into a neat ponytail, a look she thought resembled a librarian. Her big, brown eyes glistened with excitement.

Jase donned a red cape, a black hat, and a sword, which doubled as a magician's wand in this case. He began with a tap on the wooden floor. "Ladies and gentlemen," Jase shouted, "it is my distinct privilege to present to you tonight the Incredible Jodi Spencer! Take it away, Jode!"

At that, Jodi pulled *The Adventures of Hank, the Cowdog* out from behind her back and flashed it for her audience to ogle.

Chapter One: *Celebration*

Complimentary gasps came from Mom and Dad, who thought some magic trick was to follow—the book would disappear, something amazing would fall out of it, or whatever else their children's imaginations might conjure up.

Instead, she opened the book, and with an air of confidence unequaled in her experience, Jodi Spencer began to read. At first, her parents thought she was reciting yet another book; after all, her little mind was like a steel trap. They were impressed, but this was nothing new. Yet after a few pages, they began to realize that this was not mere memorization. No, Jodi was reading. *Really* reading! When she finished the first chapter, she looked up at her audience. Jase was beaming, but tears were streaming down her parents' cheeks. "What's wrong, Mama?" Jodi asked with concern in her voice.

"Oh, honey," her mom responded, "Daddy and I are so proud of you. Congratulations, Jodi! You are the best six-year-old reader I've ever known!" At that she ran to Jodi and hugged her tightly, kissing her little cheeks over and over. Her dad joined them in an exuberant embrace.

"Mama, Jase taught me!" Jodi exclaimed.

"Congratulations to you too, Jase!" their dad said, reaching to bring him into the celebration. "You've helped your sister learn the most important skill she'll ever acquire."

It was an incredible evening in the Spencers' home, one they never forgot. And Jodi read three full chapters before she tired of her performance. Her teacher was elated as well when she repeated the demonstration for her whole class. They all applauded her!

Jodi Spencer never tired of reading, but more importantly, she never forgot the love of her big brother, who sacrificed so much for her sake.

Love can accomplish things that expertise cannot. And those who love enough to believe in others should always be congratulated for doing so.

2 S A M U E L 6 : 2 1

"I will celebrate

before the LORD.*"*

15

Dream lofty dreams,

and as you dream, so shall you become.

Your vision is the promise

of what you shall at last unveil.

— John Ruskin

Celebration

Outstanding

Number One

Gratitude

Remembrance

Affirmation

Treasure

Success

CHAPTER 2

Outstanding

It's not often enough that accomplishments receive praise. Frequently, our devoted time and hard work go unnoticed and unappreciated. After all, working hard is just a part of life. But this time your efforts can't be overlooked. I am proud of you. You've done your best, and it shows.

Two thumbs up, a round of applause, a standing ovation. It needs to be said: You've done an outstanding job.

P S A L M 9 : 1

I will **praise** you,

O LORD, with all my heart;

I will **tell** of all your **wonders.**

What we are is

God's gift to us.

What we become

is our gift to God.

—*Eleanor Powell*

22

The Upside-Down Letter

Marcus was seven years old and African-American. He lived in what writer Anne Rivers Siddons called the "treacherous South" in a time when racism was served up at Southern tables like cornbread and dumplings.

It was time for the annual Christmas program at the local elementary school. Marcus was cast as the holder of the *T* in the letter lineup that spelled out MERRY CHRISTMAS. Sharon Vincent won the coveted role of Mary, the mother of Jesus. To the aggravation of her brothers and sisters, she made a nightly ritual of posing and primping in front of the mirror in the costume her mother had made her. Then she'd spend the rest of the evening shushing her brothers and sisters as she rehearsed in the living room until bedtime. As the day of the scheduled performance approached, her brothers and sisters tired of her movie-star behavior and were eager to get the play over with. Sharon's mother, Betty, worried that her children would be so annoyed with Sharon that they would miss the whole meaning of the Christmas drama.

The night of the program arrived, and the weather was bitterly cold and snowy. Betty bundled her five children up and headed to the school. "Why do we have to go?" "How long will it last?" "Do we have to hug Sharon after it's over?" "Mama, don't let them talk when I'm onstage!" Betty fielded her children's comments for the duration of the ride to what should have been one of the most meaningful nights of the holiday season. *How can I turn this night around and make this a night they will remember for more than Sharon's attitude and the bad weather?* thought Betty.

Sharon was whisked off to put on her costume as Betty and her other children found seats in the middle of the auditorium. The curtain opened to twenty-five brave children all decked out as shepherds, wise men, angels, and an assortment of barnyard animals. They struggled through their lines but managed to bring the familiar story of Christ's birth to life. Sharon did perform splendidly. All her practice had paid off, and as much as they hated to admit it, her siblings were truly proud of her. They applauded loudly as Sharon took her bow.

It was now time for the finale, the string of youngsters spelling out the seasonal greeting. This was Marcus's big moment. But unbeknownst to him his letter was upside down. The audience roared, finding his mistake incredibly amusing. But Betty was shocked at the behavior of the audience and hushed her children, who had also begun to snicker. Betty's heart went out to Marcus as his face melted into a mask of humiliation. The laughter came because of his letter being upside down, but he thought they were laughing at him— because he was black. The laughter went on too long, and the boy was close to tears.

As the curtain closed, Betty motioned to her children to follow her, and they all quickly disappeared through a side door next to the stage. Thinking they were being hurried off to congratulate Sharon, the children looked everywhere for their sister.

"There she is, Mama," one of the children said.

"We'll see her in a minute," Betty said as she made her way through the maze of children and parents.

Puzzled, the children followed their mother right up to the little boy who sat waiting in the wings for parents. Betty bent down until she was eye-level with

Chapter Two: *Outstanding*

Marcus and gently took his hand. She spoke in a strong and encouraging voice: "You did a wonderful job out there. I want you to know that the audience wasn't laughing at you. They were laughing at your letter. It was turned upside down." Betty picked up the letter and showed Marcus the problem. "You, Marcus, were outstanding."

Sharon had looked around until she found her family surrounding her classmate. She joined them as they congratulated Marcus on his performance. Realizing the importance of the moment, she, too, bragged on the grateful little boy. A smile slowly formed on Marcus's lips, and he thanked them all. Betty had done it. She managed to make the night a night to remember, especially for a little boy named Marcus.

Circumstances are just raw material out of which God makes character and strength and virtue. Only through experience of trial and suffering can the soul be strengthened, vision cleared, ambition inspired, and success achieved.

—Helen Keller

Celebration

Outstanding

Number One

Gratitude

Remembrance

Affirmation

Treasure

Success

CHAPTER 3

Number One

Winning is wonderful. Achievement is exhilarating. But you'd be special even without those notches in your belt. You'll always be number one in my book.

Popular culture says, "Go for the gold!" "Just do it," "Winning is everything." Your achievement wouldn't be complete without a heartfelt congratulations, but always remember it's the person inside—the real you—that makes me shout, "You're number one!"

1 PETER 4:10

Each one should use whatever gift

he has received

to serve others, faithfully administering

God's grace in its various forms.

I attribute my success to this—

I never gave or took any excuse.

— *Florence Nightingale*

Life affords no higher pleasure

than that of surmounting difficulties,

passing from one step of

success to another,

forming new wishes

and seeing them gratified.

—Samuel
Johnson

Let us run with endurance

the race that God

has set before us.

Hebrews 12:1 NLT

Celebration

Outstanding

Number One

Gratitude

Remembrance

Affirmation

Treasure

Success

CHAPTER 4

Gratitude

A heart that makes room for gratitude is never disappointed. God sees to it that the blessings we bestow on others boomerang back to us—sometimes in unexpected ways, but always there nonetheless. An attitude of gratitude equips us to face both the mountains and the valleys of life, because we know who our Navigator is. Everything we encounter contributes to our ultimate good when we trust the journey to God.

May your happiness be complete as you give thanks for the good things He has brought your way.

JEREMIAH 33:11

Give **thanks** to the LORD Almighty,

for the LORD is good;

his love endures forever.

The unthankful heart…discovers no mercies; but let the thankful heart sweep through the day and, as the magnet finds the iron, so it will find, in every hour, some heavenly blessings!

—Henry Ward Beecher

A Friend in Time

Todd and Troy had been friends since the seventh grade. Todd, a gifted athlete, stocky and strong, was walking home from school one Friday when he saw the thin-framed Troy toting at least seven books and various items from his locker. Todd was thinking about all the activities he had planned for the weekend when he saw a group of boys come upon Troy with mischief in their eyes. They poked fun at the seemingly studious boy, knocked the books from his arms, and then ran away.

Todd, always troubled at the sight of injustice, ran to help Troy up. "Hey, my name is Todd; what's yours?" Todd said cheerfully.

"Troy is my name," came the glum response.

"Don't worry about those guys; they're a bunch of jerks. I've had a few run-ins with them myself," Todd said sympathetically. "You know, there are other things to do on the weekend besides homework. There are football games, parties, or just hangin' out with friends."

"Well, I don't have too many friends," Troy said as he walked away.

Todd caught up with him and stood in front of him. "Well, you have one now, Troy. I'll walk you home, and then we can go to the football game tonight and hang out all weekend. How does that sound?"

"I, uh, guess it sounds all right," Troy said haltingly.

The boys did spend that weekend together and every weekend after that all through high school. They participated in life together in every way two boys who are growing a union of souls can. Troy helped Todd in classes he didn't understand, and Todd helped Troy learn some basic athletic skills, which were difficult for the physically weaker boy.

They shared the heartache of being turned down by the girls they wanted to take to their first prom. They shared the hurt of losing a friend in an auto accident and staying up all night to pray and ask God to help them understand the loss. And they celebrated the day they got their driver's licenses by trading off the driving responsibilities every hour on the hour, all weekend long.

As graduation approached, they realized they would not be going to the same university. Troy, graduating with top honors in his class, had a full ride to a top-level institute for learning in the East, and Todd would be going to a state university to save money. They spent their last weekend together reliving the pains and the pleasures of their shared friendship.

Along with the top honors, Troy would be giving the valedictory speech to the whole assembly on Thursday night during the graduation ceremonies. Todd tried to get Troy to practice his speech on him, but Troy would simply say, "You will just have to wait, my friend."

As the proceedings began, anticipation filled the air for both young men. In so many ways, this night was the beginning, yet it also was the conclusion of the life they had grown accustomed to. The school principal stood and introduced Troy with well-deserved accolades.

Troy came to the microphone and began with a stammer in his voice. "On this day of congratulations and celebration, I want to express my deepest gratitude and appreciation to one particular friend—Todd Adams. Would you come up here and join me, Todd?" A visibly stunned Todd stood slowly and walked up the aisle to stand right next to Troy.

Troy began with emotion in his voice. "Todd doesn't know it, but he is the reason I stand here today. Six years ago Todd Adams met me on the street. My arms were full of books, and my heart was full of hurt and anxiety. He befriended me on the very day I needed a friend the most. You see, I wasn't just on the way home with an armload of books. I was on the way to take my life, and I had emptied my locker so my mother wouldn't have to do it after they found my body."

Gasps were heard from all over the auditorium. Both boys, eyes brimming with tears, faced each other. Troy put his hands on Todd's shoulders, looked him squarely in the eyes, and said, "You see, my friend, you did not simply save my weekend on that fall afternoon in seventh grade—you saved my life. It is because of you that I stand here today. Thank you, Todd. Thank you with all of my heart for being the truest of friends. What you saw that day was a boy in need; what I found was a hero of the highest order."

Todd and Troy did go to different universities, but theirs was a friendship that lasted a lifetime. They walked arm in arm through life just as they had done through their school years. Each was afforded many opportunities to be a hero to the other, and both rose up to the occasion every time.

I thank You God

for this most amazing day;

for the leaping greenly spirits

of trees and a blue true dream of sky;

and for everything which is

natural which is infinite which is yes.

—E.E. Cummings

Celebration

Outstanding

Number One

Gratitude

Remembrance

Affirmation

Treasure

Success

CHAPTER 5

Remembrance

As you take a few moments to bask in the warmth of your success, take time to recall some of your favorite or not-so-favorite memories. Think of the times when the work made you weary but determination kept your spirit strong. Remind yourself of the lessons you've learned along the way. Laugh at the mistakes that helped you grow. Bring to mind stories of your triumphs and defeats. It's good to remember the good and the bad so that no matter how high you soar, you never forget where you've come from.

1 CORINTHIANS 9:24

Run in such a way as to get the prize.

God gave us memory

that we might have

roses in December.

— Sir James
M. Barrie

Love on the Run

She giggled to herself as she attached the number to her shirt. In her wildest imagination she would never have pictured herself running in a marathon. She stretched while the cool morning breeze hitting her face brought her back to the task at hand. She pushed herself into the crowd, waiting to hear the starting gun.

When the shot rang out, she was on her way, a rush of adrenaline carrying her the first few miles. The hours gave her time to think. To remember. She began running because *he* did. First it was a way to be together and get a little exercise. After they were married, it was a planned time to enjoy the early morning hours, as well as a way to enjoy the glow of the sky as the sun peeked above the horizon. After the first five years, the early morning run became a way to stay connected. The comfortable stride they fell into became a symbol of their commitment to stay in step with each other in all areas of their lives. Sometimes a brief run in the evening air was a means to outrun the stress they dealt with as their responsibilities increased with their careers as well as the addition of the children.

She remembered the point when the goal of running became to forget. To run away. She could still hear the sound of the ambulances as she rushed into the emergency room after The Call. The day had started like all the others with a morning jog in a fine mist that had later turned into a hard rain. They had parted with "I love you" and "See you tonight." The next day she started running alone.

The early morning jog soon became a hard run to clear the fog caused by another night of listening to the clock tick and praying,

54

"God, help me to understand. Help me to keep my faith and show it to the children like he would have wanted me to."

After months, the run became a time to remember the good things. It was a selfish time to embrace the memories that helped her make it through the rest of the day. With the encouragement of friends and her children, the run became a time of training her body and mind for a marathon. She knew their encouragement was to train physically. She knew the real training for her was to face the race emotionally.

The roar of the crowd brought her back. She was nearing the end. Her friends would congratulate her for finishing the race. She would congratulate herself for crossing the finish line between "Why?" and "Why not?"

Never give in, never give in,

never, never, never, never—

in nothing, great or small, large or petty—

never give in except to convictions of honor

and good sense.

— *Winston Churchill*

Celebration

Outstanding

Number One

Gratitude

Remembrance

Affirmation

Treasure

Success

CHAPTER 6

Affirmation

How much brighter the world would be if we filled it with "yes's" rather than "no's." Your life is a visible affirmation that God still works through individuals, pouring out His goodness and tying up loose ends we thought were frayed beyond repair.

In saying "Congratulations," let me add a resounding "Yes!" to the new happiness that has come your way.

It couldn't have happened to someone nicer.

ECCLESIASTES 3:12

I know that there is nothing

better for men than

to be happy and

do good while they live.

ANYWAY

People are often unreasonable, illogical and self-centered;
Forgive them anyway.
If you are kind, people may accuse you of selfish,
ulterior motives;
Be kind anyway.
If you are successful, you will win some false friends
and true enemies;
Succeed anyway.

If you are honest and frank, they may cheat you;
    Be forthright anyway,
What you spent years building, they may destroy
    overnight;
    Build anyway.
The good you do today, they often will forget tomorrow;
    Do good anyway.
Give the world the best you have and it will
    never be enough;
    Give the world the best you've got anyway.
You see, in the final analysis, it is between you and God;
    It was never between you and them, anyway.

—Unknown

1 CHRONICLES 29:17

"I know, my God,

that you test the heart and

are pleased with integrity.

All these things have I given

willingly and

with honest intent."

Consistent, timely encouragement

has the staggering magnetic power

to draw an immortal soul to

the God of hope.

The one whose name is

Wonderful Counselor.

—Charles Swindoll

Every man's life

is a fairy tale,

written by God's fingers.

—Hans Christian Andersen

Celebration

Outstanding

Number One

Gratitude

Remembrance

Affirmation

Treasure

Success

CHAPTER 7

Treasure

This one moment in time is a gift from God, to do with all that you dream possible. Treasure it. Remember it. Use it as a catalyst for your future happiness.

To help savor the moment, try these ideas:

- Journal your thoughts about it
- Record any answers to prayer in a prayer diary
- Call a friend and share it "live"
- Bake a cake and celebrate!

DEUTERONOMY 16:15

For the LORD your God will bless you...

in all the work of your hands,

and your joy will be

complete.

If you can dream it, you can do it.

Always remember this whole thing

was started by a mouse.

— *Walt Disney*

The LORD is my shepherd;
    I have everything I need.
He lets me rest in green meadows;
    he leads me beside peaceful streams.
    He renews my strength.
He guides me along right paths,
    bringing honor to his name.
Even when I walk
    through the dark valley of death,

I will not be afraid,
    for you are close beside me.
Your rod and your staff
    protect and comfort me.
You prepare a feast for me
    in the presence of my enemies.
You welcome me as a guest,
    anointing my head with oil.
    My cup overflows with blessings.
Surely your goodness and unfailing
    love will pursue me
    all the days of my life,
and I will live in the house of the LORD
    forever.

PROVERBS 4:23

"Above all else,

guard your heart,

for it is the wellspring

of life."

When I stand before God at the end of my life,

I would hope that I would not have

a single bit of talent left and could say,

"I used everything you gave me."

—*Erma Bombeck*

Celebration

Outstanding

Number One

Gratitude

Remembrance

Affirmation

Treasure

Success

C H A P T E R   8

Success

Success is born of effort and inspiration, hard work and conviction, dedication and passion.

Though the road to success will inevitably be strewn with obstacles, it is those who push ahead with determination and unwavering faith who achieve the goal. Congratulations to you on your success!

May you always invest your heart wholly in all you do and raise your hand to God in praise for His blessings of success in your life.

NEHEMIAH 2:20

The God of heaven

will give us

success.

There is wonderful

freedom and joy

in coming to recognize that

the fun is in the becoming.

—Gloria Gaither

The Willow Tree Party

The year Melinda turned eight, she accomplished an incredible feat. She climbed the willow tree in her backyard. Climbing a willow tree certainly wouldn't seem that significant except that this tree was huge. It was gargantuan. It was a kingdom waiting to be conquered. It rivaled the tree of *Swiss Family Robinson* fame.

Melinda's mother had raised all of her children with a long tether. She never minded if they roamed the woods or swam in the pond. She would shake her head when Melinda came home with bloody knees or poison ivy, but she never said, "You'd better stay away from there." No, without knowing it, Melinda's mom taught her that a fertile imagination was more important than good grades in school—though Melinda managed to get both.

Being a tomboy meant Melinda participated in her share of death-defying feats in the woods behind her house. There she fought battles on hilltops, crossed streams on fallen logs, and scaled cliffs by clutching large roots that stuck out from the red clay.

One afternoon, as the sun was beginning to set, Melinda came tromping out of the woods for supper. She spied that gargantuan willow tree. There it sat—just inside the clearing of her backyard—close to the woods but not part of it. Its "willowy" limbs draped to the ground, forming a fort underneath where anything could hide. The trunk was stout, and Melinda reasoned that someone had planted it years ago. Melinda stared at the tree, almost daring it to call her name, challenging her to conquer it.

She had climbed willow trees before, but not this one. The branch closest to the ground had been too high for her seven-year-old legs. But today she was eight, and the thought entered her mind that maybe, just maybe, she was taller now and could reach that branch and enter the private home of the willow tree.

Melinda walked up to the trunk and strained to grasp the first branch. It was still too high, so she jumped. No luck. She jumped again. This time she grabbed the branch and hung on for dear life, only to feel her hands scrape the bark on her way down. Not ready to admit defeat, she got back up and only briefly glanced at her skinned knees and scuffed red tennis shoes.

An idea formed in Melinda's head. Many times she had seen her daddy tote water in a large metal bucket. The bucket sat in a corner of the garage, covered with cobwebs. But a few cobwebs had never stopped Melinda, and she decided it was time to put that bucket to good use.

She dragged it out to the backyard and positioned it on the most level spot she could find beneath the willow tree. One foot, then two feet. She felt the bucket wobble. But just before it turned completely over, she grabbed the branch and managed to pull herself into the "green room."

Chapter Eight: *Success*

There she was at last, sheltered by the green curtain of leaves, with no one but herself to extend congratulations for her monumental success. The wind blew softly, making the curtain rustle. She lay back on the wide branch and relished the quietude of a lazy summer day. It was a wonderful and glorious feeling.

She was eight years old.

It was her birthday.

She had done it!

People of mediocre ability

sometimes achieve outstanding

success because they don't

know when to quit.

Most [people] succeed

because they are determined to.

—George E.
Allen

I have fought a good fight, I have finished the race,

and I have remained faithful.

And now the prize awaits me—

the crown of righteousness that the Lord,

the righteous Judge,

will give me on that great day of his return.

2 Timothy 4:7–8 NLT